Founder's Frequency Code

Decode Success with Astrology, Numerology, Vastu & Rituals

Shantulya Saini

SPI PUBLICATIONS

Published by **SPI Publications**, www.spipublications.in

SPI, the **SPI logo**, and **Split Poetry India** are trademarks of **SPI Publications**, or its affiliates.

ISBN-13: 978-81-990408-4-7

First Edition 2025

SPI Publications

Corporate & Editorial Office

117/2, Sector 37, Khandsa Road,
Gurgaon, Haryana 122 001
Phone: +91 98355 52940
Email: contact@spipublications.in
Website: www.spipublications.in

Processed and Printed in India

Founder's Frequency Code

Decode Success with Astrology, Numerology, Vastu & Rituals

Copyright

Founder's Frequency Code
Decode Success with Astrology, Numerology, Vastu & Rituals

This book is a work of nonfiction inspired by real consultations, research, and spiritual frameworks. All case studies are anonymized or fictionalized for privacy and illustrative clarity.

First Edition: 2025
Published in India

Contact:
Email: shantul5@gmail.com
📞 WhatsApp: +91 8619041996
Instagram: @Shantulya
Website: www.iimproveedge.com

Table of Contents

Preface

Entrepreneurship is a sacred path.
Yet for decades, we've treated it as only a logical game — a world of pitches, profits, and performance metrics.

As someone who walked both worlds — from elite education to spiritual transformation — I saw a gap no one was talking about:
Energy. Frequency. Alignment.
Not just in personal life, but in startups, sales, visibility, and success itself.

Founder's Frequency Code was born from this space — a toolkit, a lens, and a map for those who feel called to build not just businesses, but soul-aligned empires.

This book is not a formula. It is a frequency reset — a way to build your startup, team, brand, and self from inner truth.

Whether you're scaling your venture or still nurturing a seed of an idea — may this book be a guide that speaks to your soul as much as your strategy.

With intention and love,
— Shantulya Saini

About the Author

Shantulya Saini is a spiritual strategist, Vedic astrologer, and founder of IIMprove Edge — a platform dedicated to education, energetic alignment, and soul-led entrepreneurship.

An alumnus of IIM Ahmedabad, with a BTech–MTech in Electronics & Communication Engineering, Shantulya began his career as an IT professional. But his deeper passion for human potential led him to transition into the education sector, where he spent over 18 years teaching and mentoring thousands of students for CAT, IIT-JEE, and competitive exams.

Along the way, he immersed himself in Vedic astrology, numerology, and Vastu Shastra, eventually merging ancient sciences with modern success strategy.

Today, he works as an energetic consultant and horoscope reader, guiding clients across India and abroad. His consultations help entrepreneurs, founders, and professionals decode their life patterns, business timing, wealth blocks, and inner clarity.

Whether it's choosing a cofounder, naming a business, aligning office space, or launching during the right planetary phase — Shantulya's approach combines spiritual depth with strategic precision.

His mission is simple yet powerful:
"Align energy before effort — and success becomes soulful, scalable, and sustainable."

Email: shantul5@gmail.com
📞 WhatsApp: +91 8619041996
Instagram: @Shantulya
Website: www.iimproveedge.com

Founder's Frequency Code: -

Decode Success with Astrology, Numerology, Vastu & Rituals

📘 Chapter 1: Why Founder Compatibility is Destiny

Subheading: The Energetic Roots of Every Startup Success or Struggle

"Startups don't break down because of bad ideas.
They collapse when energetic alignment between founders is ignored."
— *Shantulya Saini*

The Illusion of "Just Find a Cofounder"

We live in a world that glorifies hustle, bootstrapping, pitch decks, and scale. The startup narrative is driven by ideas, MVPs, investors, exits — and somewhere lost in that storm is the energy that runs all of it: **the founders themselves.**

Every startup begins with a spark — two or more people united by passion. But soon, the cracks appear:

- Disagreements over direction
- Ego battles about visibility
- Differing working styles
- A slow, silent drift into resentment

And yet, none of this shows up on the cap table. None of this is asked in a startup accelerator pitch.

"Are you vibrationally compatible with your cofounder?"
No one asks it. But they should.
Because your cofounder is **your karmic mirror.**

💡 What Most Founders Ignore

In early-stage startups, cofounders often:

- Choose friends over functional matches
- Prioritize shared vision but ignore emotional behavior
- Split equity without exploring conflict styles
- Dismiss intuition in favor of logic

This is where **spiritual intelligence** must enter.

What if we approached cofounding like a sacred energetic agreement — just like a marriage?

✋ Story: The Startup That Collapsed in Silence

Let's meet Ankita and Rohit.
Both passionate engineers. Both committed to building a mental health platform in India.

The idea was perfect.
The funding came.
But within 10 months:

- Rohit ghosted for weeks at a time
- Ankita made major decisions solo
- They avoided difficult conversations
- Burnout set in

When I was brought in as an energy consultant, the issue wasn't product or users — it was energetic mismatch.

Their charts revealed:

- Rohit was in **Rahu Maha Dasha** (illusion, ego, instability)
- Ankita had a **Moon-Rahu affliction**, making her emotionally volatile
- Their Life Path Numbers (8 and 3) clashed — **control vs. freedom**

There was no ritual. No framework. No boundary.
The business died. But the **lesson was born**.

🧘 Cofounder = Karmic Contract

In Vedic astrology, **the 7th house** rules:

1. Marriage
2. Contracts
3. Open enemies

Yes — cofounders can evolve into *enemies* if the energy isn't managed consciously.

A cofounder is not just a partner. They are the **spiritual mirror of your current growth phase.**

If you ignore your emotional blind spots, your business will magnify them.

🧭 Six Energetic Areas to Align Before Building Together

Area	Key Question to Ask
Emotional Energy	How do we each react under pressure?
Spiritual Awareness	Do we both value inner work and growth?
Communication Rhythm	Do we talk daily or disappear for days?
Decision Process	Is one impulsive, the other overthinking?
Vision Horizon	Do we want the same destination and speed?
Dasha Cycles (Astro)	Are our planetary periods flowing or clashing?

✅ If 4 or more answers are mismatched — pause before signing that equity split.

🔢 Quick Compatibility Guide

📅 Numerology + Astrology Combo

Step 1: Get both founders' full birth details

Step 2: Check Moon Sign compatibility

Step 3: Calculate Life Path Numbers

How to calculate Life Path:
DD + MM + YYYY → Reduce to 1 digit
E.g., 24/03/1986 → 2 + 4 + 0 + 3 + 1 + 9 + 8 + 6 = **33 → 6**

Life Path	Founder Energy	Best Partners	Conflict With
1	Leader, Solo Driver	3, 5, 9	2, 8
2	Sensitive, Harmonizer	6, 8, 9	1, 5
3	Creative, Communicator	1, 5, 6	4, 8
4	Planner, Disciplined	2, 7, 8	3, 5
5	Dynamic, Fast-changer	1, 3, 6	4, 7
6	Nurturer, Harmonizer	2, 3, 9	1, 8
7	Spiritual, Deep Thinker	2, 4, 9	5, 8
8	Strategic, Power-driven	2, 4, 6	1, 3, 7
9	Visionary, Selfless	1, 3, 6	4, 8

Also check **Dasha Periods**:
If one is under **Rahu**, other under **Shani**, major friction arises.
Ideal: At least one founder in **Jupiter** or **Venus** phase.

💡 Story: A Startup That Scaled in Harmony

Let's meet **Shruti and Aman**.
They weren't best friends, but they were energetically aligned.

1. Shruti: Moon in **Taurus**, Life Path 6 — calm, nurturing
2. Aman: Moon in **Cancer**, Life Path 2 — intuitive, diplomatic

3. Both were in **Saturn Mahadasha** — discipline, structure

They meditated together every Friday, spoke gratitude aloud, and resolved conflicts with intention.

Result? 3 years in, they hadn't raised funding, but had doubled revenue every year and built a peaceful, loyal team.

Rituals to Align Founders Spiritually

1. **Weekly Vision Ritual**
   Every Friday, sit in silence. Speak your startup dream aloud.
2. **Mutual Gratitude Sharing**
   Every Sunday, share 3 things you appreciate in each other.
3. **Conflict Cleanup Chant**
   Light a diya after any major disagreement. Say:

"I honor the soul before me; beyond the role they play."
Sit in silence for 3 minutes.

Red Flags: Time to Recalibrate or Exit?

1. You feel **drained** before meetings
2. You **hide your wins** to avoid jealousy
3. Communication feels **strategic, not soulful**
4. You secretly wish you were doing it **solo**

Don't force-fit spiritual misalignment.
Recalibrate or exit gracefully.

✅ Founder Fit Checklist

Question	Yes / No
Have we discussed our emotional reactions?	
Do our Moon signs and Life Paths complement each other?	
Are our planetary Dashas stable or supportive?	
Do we believe in conflict healing, not just avoiding?	
Are we aligned on success definitions and timelines?	
Can we speak to each other's soul, not just strategy?	

✔ **5–6 Yes** = Aligned
⚠ **3–4 Yes** = Do the spiritual work
✕ **2 or less** = Pause. Reevaluate.

💥 Final Wisdom

"The universe sends us cofounders not to complete our startups — but to complete our inner work."

Founders who are energetically aligned:

1. Make fewer, wiser decisions
2. Fight less, build more
3. Attract the right investors and team
4. Grow personally while growing professionally

Your startup is not just a company.
It's your karmic classroom.
Choose your cofounder like you'd choose your soul mirror.

📕 Chapter 2: The Compatibility Decoder

Subheading: Moon Signs, Life Paths & Planetary Phases That Define Cofounder Chemistry

"Vision brings people together.
But energy decides if they stay together."
— *Shantulya Saini*

🌐 The Founder Compatibility Triangle

Before building a company together, check if your **energies are in harmony** across these 3 lenses:

-

◆ **Moon Sign → Emotional frequency**

◆ **Life Path Number → Core mission & personality**

◆ **Dasha Period (Planetary Phase) → Timing + behavior lens**

These three layers **define your founder chemistry**, conflicts, and soul contract.

🧠 Why Compatibility Needs Decoding, Not Guessing

Founders are often chosen for:

1. Shared vision
2. Friendship or past connection
3. Complementary skills

But these don't guarantee energetic alignment.

Time and again, promising startups dissolve not from external failure — but from **unseen energetic friction** between founders.

Energetic decoding is the **user research of partnerships.**
Do it before investing your soul, not just your savings.

🌓 Step 1: Decode Emotional Compatibility with Moon Signs

Your **Moon Sign** (Chandra Rashi) governs:

1. Stress response
2. Inner rhythm
3. Emotional needs
4. Comfort zone

It's more revealing than Sun sign for daily behavior.

🪐 Moon Sign Combinations: Emotional Chemistry Chart

Moon Sign	Best Emotional Matches	Caution With
Aries	Leo, Sagittarius, Aquarius	Cancer, Virgo
Taurus	Virgo, Capricorn, Cancer	Aquarius, Leo
Gemini	Libra, Aquarius, Aries	Scorpio, Taurus
Cancer	Pisces, Taurus, Scorpio	Aries, Gemini
Leo	Aries, Sagittarius, Libra	Taurus, Capricorn
Virgo	Capricorn, Taurus, Pisces	Aries, Gemini
Libra	Gemini, Aquarius, Leo	Virgo, Cancer
Scorpio	Cancer, Pisces, Virgo	Gemini, Sagittarius
Sagittarius	Aries, Leo, Aquarius	Cancer, Scorpio
Capricorn	Taurus, Virgo, Pisces	Leo, Aries
Aquarius	Libra, Gemini, Sagittarius	Taurus, Cancer
Pisces	Cancer, Scorpio, Capricorn	Leo, Aries

💡 **Case Study: Aarav & Neha**

1. **Aarav**: Gemini Moon — fast, ideas-first, playful
2. **Neha**: Scorpio Moon — deep, intense, structure-loving

They were drawn to contrast... but soon:

1. Aarav kept pivoting
2. Neha needed emotional depth
3. They began avoiding real conversations

🧠 Solution:
After understanding their charts, they **reassigned roles**:
Aarav → Innovation + fundraising
Neha → Execution + quality

Result? **Harmony improved. Business stabilized.**

🔢 **Step 2: Decode Life Path Numbers — Your Soul Blueprint**

🌟 **What is a Life Path Number?**

It's the **vibrational frequency of your life's purpose**, based on your full birthdate.

Reveals how you:

1. Make decisions
2. Handle power
3. Navigate conflict
4. Create value

🧮 **How to Calculate**

24 March 1986 → 2+4+0+3+1+9+8+6 = 33 → Master Number

Reduce to single digit only if not 11, 22, or 33.
These are **Master Builders** — hold extra karmic energy.

🧬 Life Path Compatibility Table

Life Path	Personality	Best Matches	Conflict With
1	Initiator, assertive	3, 5, 9	2, 8
2	Diplomatic, sensitive	4, 6, 9	1, 5
3	Creative, expressive	1, 5, 6	4, 8
4	Structured, logical	2, 6, 8	3, 5
5	Adventurous, quick	1, 3, 6	4, 7
6	Harmonizer, nurturing	2, 3, 9	1, 8
7	Spiritual, reserved	4, 9, 2	5, 8
8	Power-driven, bold	2, 4, 6	1, 3, 7
9	Idealistic, mission-led	2, 3, 6	4, 8
11/22/33	Visionary builders	2, 6, 9	Need calm energy

💡 Case Study: Kunal (1) & Ishita (8)

1. Kunal: Bold, solo-style leader
2. Ishita: Strategic, execution-focused

Clash: Both wanted control
Fix:

1. Clear role ownership
2. A 3rd mentor added for energetic neutrality
   Result: Less ego war, more clarity

🪐 Step 3: Check Dasha Period Alignment

Every 6–20 years, we go through **Planetary Mahadashas** — cosmic phases that shape behavior and karma.

Dasha	Energy Vibe	Business Impact
Jupiter	Wisdom, expansion	Best for starting, scaling
Venus	Harmony, attraction	Ideal for branding, community
Sun	Power, fame	Good for visibility, PR
Saturn	Discipline, delays	Long-term, operations
Rahu	Chaos, illusion	Fame + burnout risk — be cautious
Ketu	Withdrawal, detachment	Need simplicity + soul clarity
Mercury	Logic, agility	Great for early stage + innovation
Moon	Emotion, reflection	Works well for intuition-based biz
Mars	Action, risk	Good for scale and drive

⚠️ Rahu + Shani in opposite Dashas = Conflict
✅ Jupiter + Venus in synergy = Flow

💡 Bonus Case Study: Riya & Dev

1. Riya: Moon in Taurus, Life Path 6, Jupiter Dasha
2. Dev: Moon in Pisces, Life Path 2, Venus Dasha

They were not just compatible — their **timing aligned perfectly**.

They launched a wellness startup and hit ₹1 crore in sales in 14 months — with no fights and zero team attrition.

❓ What If Your Compatibility Is Low?

It doesn't always mean the partnership must end. Try:

1. **Energetic role swaps**: Vision vs. Execution
2. **Spiritual advisor/mentor** as a balancing 3rd force
3. **Conflict rituals** and gratitude routines
4. **Delay major decisions** if Dashas are unstable
5. Create a **Cofounder Energetic Agreement**

💡 Cofounder Rituals to Stay Aligned

1. **Monday Morning Energy Check**
    1. 1 feeling, 1 win, 1 block
    2. Silent 1-min breath together
2. **Dasha Sync Calendar**
    1. Mark both Dasha transitions
    2. Avoid big launches during major shifts
3. **Founder's Friday Light Ritual**
    1. Light a diya, say vision aloud weekly
    2. Reset energy field intentionally

🧾 Founder Fit Compatibility Scorecard

Parameter	Score (1–10)
Moon Sign Match	
Life Path Complement	
Dasha Harmony	
Conflict Resolution Style	
Ritual & Alignment Practice	
Emotional Trust & Safety	

Total / 60
✔ 50+ = Strong Green Light
⚠ 30–50 = Mixed — needs alignment work
❌ Below 30 = Rethink, revisit foundation

💥 Final Wisdom

"Decode your cofounder like you would decode your market — with humility, honesty, and curiosity."

When you know someone's energetic map, you stop judging them.
You **understand them**.

Those understanding builds **trust**, and trust builds startups that last.

📕 Chapter 3: Name is Fame

Subheading: How to Align Your Business Name with Cosmic Frequency & Attraction Energy

"Your business name is not just branding.
It's your vibrational calling card to the universse."
— *Shantulya Saini*

? Why Names Aren't Just Names

Most founders spend days brainstorming their startup name based on:

1. Trends
2. Domain availability
3. Branding "coolness"

But they miss the most powerful dimension — **vibration**.

Just like a mantra, a name **emits frequency**. It holds:

1. **Numerological weight**
2. **Sound energy**
3. **Karmic invitation**

A misaligned name silently blocks money, clients, or momentum — no matter how good your product is.

🧠 A Real-World Case: When a Name Blocked Flow

A female founder approached me with her education startup "Eduxel."
It had a sleek logo, working team, decent social media, but still:

1. Enrollment remained stuck at 10–15 students/month
2. Collaborations kept breaking down
3. Her team reported "strange energy" around branding

I calculated her business name:

1. **Chaldean Value**: 13
2. **Name Total**: 13 → 4 (obstacle, rebellion, karmic correction)

Solution:

We renamed it to **"Learnova"**, vibrating to **24 (6)** — the number for harmony, Venus, attraction.

Within **60 days**:

1. Enrollments tripled
2. She was invited to speak at 2 podcasts
3. A new investor got in touch organically

Her strategy didn't change. Her **frequency** did.

🔠 Chaldean Numerology & Business Name Alignment

How it Works:

Every alphabet holds a numeric value in the **Chaldean system**, the most spiritually accurate name-number model.

🧪 Example 1: Edge

1. E = 5
2. D = 4
3. G = 3
4. E = 5

Total = 5 + 4 + 3 + 5 = 17 → 1 + 7 = 8

🔮 **Vibration = 8** → Power, control, success, finances, long-term growth

---

🧪 Example 2: Quantiva

1. Q = 1
2. U = 6
3. A = 1
4. N = 5
5. T = 4
6. I = 1
7. V = 6
8. A = 1

Total = 1 + 6 + 1 + 5 + 4 + 1 + 6 + 1 = 25 → 2 + 5 = 7

🧠 **Vibration = 7** → Deep thinking, spiritual business, research focus
✅ Suitable for education, healing, niche coaching

📅 Table: Alphabet & Chaldean Values

Letter	Value
A, I, J, Q, Y	1
B, K, R	2
C, G, L, S	3
D, M, T	4
E, N, H	5
U, V, W, X	6
O, Z	7
F, P	8

🔢 Business Name Frequencies & Their Meaning

Number	Vibration Theme	Best For Businesses That...
1	Leadership, innovation	Personal brands, startups with solo founders
2	Partnership, diplomacy	Coaching, HR, healing, NGOs
3	Expression, joy	Media, content, training
4	Structure, stability	Legal, tech, education, compliance
5	Movement, change	Travel, tech, disruptive innovation
6	Beauty, love, balance	Wellness, fashion, female-led ventures
7	Spirituality, mysticism	Research, metaphysics, niche coaching
8	Power, wealth, control	Finance, real estate, empire building
9	Service, impact	Purpose-driven, non-profit, transformation

❓ What If My Current Business Name is Misaligned?

Don't panic. You don't always need a complete rebrand. Instead:

✅ Try These Remedies:

1. **Add or adjust suffixes/prefixes**
   e.g., "Zenva" → "Zenva Edge" (adds 5+4 = 9 — impact)
2. **Recolor your branding**
   Each number has a power color. Use it in logos, banners, clothes.
   1. 1 → Red
   2. 2 → White or Light Blue
   3. 6 → Rose Pink or Light Green
   4. 8 → Deep Blue or Dark Gray

3. **Activate the name with mantra energy**
    1. Write the name 108 times for 21 days
    2. Chant "OM KLEEM [business name]" with a diya lit every Friday
4. **Align your launch days or email triggers**
   Use number-aligned dates for product drops, emails, or events

---

🧪 Business Name Energy Booster Formula

Sound Energy

1. **Chaldean Alignment**
2. **Visual Vibe (Color/Symbol)**
3. **Planetary Support**
   = Name Frequency Activation

Use this as a checklist when brainstorming or evaluating a name.

✨ Affirmation to Close the Chapter

"My business name is a mantra of abundance.
It vibrates clarity, magnetism, and divine support.
Every time it's spoken, it calls success closer."

Let this become your founding frequency.

📘 Chapter 4: Money Alignment

Subheading: Unlocking Wealth Flow Through Energetic Resonance

"Money doesn't respond to logic.
It responds to frequency."
— *Shantulya Saini*

💰 Money Is Energy, Not Math

Most founders chase money through:

1. Marketing funnels
2. Funding decks
3. Upsells and offers

And while those are important, they miss the **invisible layer**:
→ *The vibrational alignment between you and wealth.*

In Vedic tradition and universal law:

1. Money flows where **respect** flows
2. Money flows where **energy is clear**
3. Money flows where **you feel safe receiving**

Your business account is a **mirror** of your energy patterns.

💡 Real Story: The Delayed Payment Loop

One founder I worked with ran a high-quality design studio. Her clients loved her work, but:

1. Invoices were often delayed
2. Launches got stuck
3. One client ghosted after a ₹75,000 deal

When we analyzed her energy:

1. **Her chart**: Under Saturn–Ketu Dasha (blockage, detachment)
2. **Office Vastu**: Locker placed in **southeast** (fire zone — burns money)

3. **Pricing**: Offered services at ₹299, ₹599 — both **2 vibrations** (emotional, not stable)

Remedies We Applied:

1. Shifted locker to the **North direction**
2. Placed **Shree Yantra** + 5 Gomti Chakras
3. Changed pricing to ₹379 (→ 3+7+9 = 19 → 1 → leadership)
4. Started **Friday offerings** to Mahalakshmi

✅ Result in 6 weeks:

1. First ₹5L month
2. One client paid upfront for 12 months
3. She reported feeling "unstuck" for the first time in years

Your money blocks aren't about skills.
They're about **energetic clutter**.

🔢 Numerology & Money Vibration Table

Every number holds a specific frequency with money. Use this to guide:

1. Pricing
2. Invoicing
3. Package names
4. Donation or discount values

Number	Money Vibe	Best Use In...
1	Leadership, premium	Coaching, consulting, solo founders
2	Emotional, passive	Healing, donations, soft sales
3	Creative, joyful	Events, group programs, workshops
4	Stability, delays	Legal, compliance, back end ops
5	Expansion, viral	Tech products, launches, ads

Number	Money Vibe	Best Use In...
6	Luxury, feminine	Beauty, wellness, home decor
7	Spiritual, inward	Inner work, niche learning
8	Power, money magnet	Real estate, finance, long-term scale
9	Service, letting go	Free gifts, community offers

📅 Quick Pricing Fix Checklist

Before you launch or invoice, ask:

✅ Does this price reduce to 1, 5, 6, or 8? (best money vibes)
✅ Does it feel **emotionally safe** and confident to say aloud?
✅ Is it aligned with your **Life Path Number** or Business Name Vibration?

Example:
Instead of ₹299 → Try ₹379 (vibration = 1)
Instead of ₹444 → Try ₹549 (vibration = 9 → may be donation-based)

🏠 Vastu & Space: Wealth Zones Matter

In your home or office, money energy flows best when:

1. Locker is placed in the **North** or **Northeast**
2. Avoid placing safe or wallet in **Southeast** (fire) or **Southwest** (drain)
3. Place a **mirror** near cash area to symbolically double wealth

---

💰 Lakshmi Locker Ritual

Perform this once a month — preferably on a **Friday** or **Full Moon**.

🪔 Steps:

1. Clean your locker or wallet with salt water (externally)
2. Place a **red cloth** inside

3. Add:
    1. 5 **Gomti Chakras**
    2. 1 **cowrie shell**
    3. A small photo of **Lakshmi or Shree Yantra**
4. Place a note:

"I honor the energy of abundance. This locker only holds wealth that flows with grace and purpose."

5. Light a diya and chant:

"Om Shreem Mahalakshmyai Namah" (108x5)

? Behavioral Wealth Practices

Money alignment isn't just spiritual — it's emotional and behavioral:

✅ Do:

1. Express gratitude for small inflows
2. Keep ₹1001 in wallet as "seed of prosperity"
3. Use high-vibe words: "flow," "circulation," "abundance"

❌ Don't:

1. Say "I can't afford" — say "It's not aligned right now"
2. Mix business money with personal expenses
3. Undervalue your offer out of guilt

💫 Closing Affirmation

"I am open to receiving wealth that is aligned with my soul.
I release all blocks to prosperity.
My work is sacred, and I am worthy of overflow."

Money is not your enemy.
It is your **ally in expansion**, waiting to flow where the energy is clear.

📕 Chapter 5: Vastu for Visibility & Magnetism

Subheading: Designing Your Workspace to Attract Flow, Fame & Focus

"Your business is not built in a vacuum.
It grows in a space that either amplifies or blocks your energy."
— *Shantulya Saini*

🏠 Vastu = Vibrational Architecture

Most people think Vastu is only about home direction and temple placement.
But in reality, **Vastu is the science of energetic flow in space**.

In ancient India, kings-built palaces aligned to cosmic energy.
Today, as founders, our **workspace** is our modern palace.
If it blocks life force — **money slows, visibility dims, clarity fades.**

When your space is aligned, results accelerate — with less effort.

🧭 Business Vastu Map: Direction & Function

Here's how each direction impacts your startup flow:

Direction	Vastu Energy Zone	Ideal Use
North	Flow of money	Locker, incoming payments, client desk
Northeast	Vision & clarity	Meditation zone, vision board, ideas
East	Communication, new energy	Entry gate, team meetings, exposure
Southeast	Fire & action	Pantry, appliances, avoid locker here
South	Fame & discipline	Founder chair, branding, achievements
Southwest	Stability & grounding	Heavy items, CEO seat, leadership
West	Profits, networking	Team collaboration, joint ventures
Northwest	Support & motion	Guest chairs, assistants, air flow

Your **founder desk** is best placed in **Southwest** (power seat), facing **North or East**.

💡 Real Case: When Direction Changed the Game

A startup founder felt constantly blocked. Her clients would ghost, and leads felt lifeless. On analysis:

1. **Her desk faced a blank wall** in the **Southeast (fire)** direction
2. The **locker was in the Southwest** — against stability flow
3. **No sunlight** entered the office

We shifted:

1. Her desk to **Southwest**, facing **North**
2. Placed **mirror + bamboo plant** in the East
3. Added **Shree Yantra** in North
4. Activated entry with **yellow flowers** on Monday mornings

✅ Within 3 weeks:

1. Closed 2 pending deals
2. Her team felt "mentally clear"
3. She said: *"My office feels alive now."*

Just like we align chakras, we must align rooms.
Your office has an aura too.

✕ Common Vastu Mistakes That Block Success

Mistake	What It Does
Locker in Southeast	Burns money, constant cash outflow
Desk back to door or wall	No support, anxiety, betrayal from team
Toilet in North	Flushes wealth & opportunities
Clutter in Northeast	Vision blocked, confusion, unclear goals
Open shelves in Southwest	Instability, no grounding
Sharp metal objects in East	Communication breakdown, PR failure

Clean up these zones to unblock **hidden resistance.**

Founder Desk Energizing Ritual

Once a week (ideal: **Monday sunrise** or **Friday sunrise**), align your desk space with this ritual:

Steps:

1. Wipe desk surface with **salt water + lavender oil**
2. Place a **Shree Yantra** or **Clear Quartz** facing North
3. Light a diya or candle
4. Say aloud:

"This space attracts wisdom, clarity, and right action. I release all energetic clutter."

5. Keep a fresh flower or basil (Tulsi) leaf in the East corner

This clears stagnation and brings **visibility magnetism**.

Bonus Vastu Remedies for Founders

1. **North locker + gold coin inside** = wealth invitation
2. **Shankh (conch) in Northeast** = clarity & intuition
3. **Jade plant or bamboo in East** = fresh growth

4. **Cowry shells + red cloth in wallet** = protective money shield
5. **Keep logo on South wall** = strengthens brand energy

✨ Affirmation to Close the Chapter

"My space is a silent supporter of my mission.
As I align my surroundings, the universe aligns with me.
I am seen. I am supported. I am successful."

📕 Chapter 6: Client Attraction Frequency

Subheading: How to Call in Aligned Clients Through Vibration, Not Persuasion

"Your clients don't choose you because of your pitch.
They choose you because of your frequency."
— *Shantulya Saini*

🧲 Clients Are Energetic Mirrors

Every client that shows up in your business — flaky or faithful, stuck or ready — is **reflecting something in your energy field**.

If you attract:

1. People who delay payments
2. Clients who ghost after discovery calls
3. Leads that say "I'll think about it..."
   Then the work isn't just in your marketing — it's in your **magnetic field**.

You don't chase aligned clients.
You *clear space* for them to find you.

💡 Real-Life Story: The Blocked Field

Ritika was a self-love coach with a powerful message.
But her calendar was filled with:

1. Non-paying "trial" seekers
2. People who loved her content but didn't buy
3. Clients who resisted change or ghosted after 1 call

She was exhausted.

Energetic Diagnosis:

1. Her **personal belief**: "I don't know if I'm worth this."
2. Her **offer**: Priced at ₹2,222 (vibration = 8, but her Life Path = 2 → disharmony)
3. Her **space**: Past client files still open in her emails — unhealed energy cords

Frequency Fix:

1. Shifted her core affirmation to:

"I am a magnet for committed, aligned souls."

2. Repriced her offer to ₹5,555 (vibration = 1 = leadership)
3. Did a **Client Cord Cutting Ritual** (see below)
4. Added "ready-to-invest" filter questions to her lead form

✅ Result: Within 14 days, she signed 3 clients — one paid in full for 3 months.

🔎 The Client Frequency Audit

Use this table to identify & shift subconscious client blocks:

Blocked Belief	**What You Attract**	**Shift to…**
"People don't want to pay me."	Ghosting, freebie-seekers	"Aligned souls value my presence & price."
"I need to convince them to buy."	Resistant energy, confusion	"My energy invites, not chases."
"I can help everyone."	Mismatch, burnout	"I serve those divinely aligned with me."
"If I charge more, people will leave."	Insecure clients, guilt pricing	"I charge in honor of both me and them."
"I must overdeliver to prove I'm worthy."	Draining clients, imbalance	"I serve with grace, not overcompensation."

🧘 Reflect on which belief lives in your system. Then rewrite it.

✨ Client Attraction Ritual

Do this every **Friday night** (Venus = attraction) or **new moon** (fresh energy).

Steps:

1. Sit in a quiet space. Light a white candle or diya.
2. Write:

"I now call-in clients who are ready, respectful, and aligned with my soul work."

3. Burn incense (if possible) — rose, lavender, or frankincense
4. Chant:

"Om Kleem Shreem Swaha" (108x3)
(Kleem = attraction; Shreem = abundance)

5. Bless your phone or client booking calendar with a flower
6. Place your note on your altar or in your workspace

This activates a clear, receptive frequency field.
The shift may start within hours... or unfold in the weeks ahead.

Affirmation Bank for Client Magnetism

Read or write 1–2 daily to align with client flow:

Daily Affirmations

"I attract soulmate clients who value, pay, and transform."

"Aligned people find me easily and feel safe to say yes."

"I don't hustle. My vibration speaks before I do."

"Every offer I create reaches the right hearts."

"I trust divine timing and energetic readiness."

Write these in your journal or post them above your desk.
The more **you believe**, the more *they* show up.

💡 Energetic Closing Checklist

Before a big launch or client intake, ask:

✅ Is my offer priced in an empowering frequency?
✅ Have I cleared past energy from mismatched clients?
✅ Does my content reflect **clarity, not confusion**?
✅ Am I open to *receive*, not just prove?

🌟 Closing Quote

"Client attraction is not about louder funnels.
It's about **clearer frequency**.
When you are ready — they are already on the way."

Let your presence speak louder than your pitch.

📘 Chapter 7: The Launch Timing Code

Subheading: Aligning Your Business Rollout with Cosmic Timing

"A good offer launched at the wrong time can feel like failure.
But the same offer launched in divine timing becomes a magnet."
— *Shantulya Saini*

⏳ Not All Time Is Equal

Modern business advice says:

1. "Just launch!"
2. "Done is better than perfect."
3. "You can't wait for the right moment."

But spiritual business wisdom says:

"**Right energy at the right time brings right results.**"

In Vedic astrology and numerology, **timing is a living force**.
Some days are charged with fire, visibility, growth.
Others are clouded with fog, resistance, or karmic testing.

As a founder, you're not just building offers —
you're planting **energetic seeds**.
And like any farmer, *season matters*.

💡 Real Story: A Launch That Waited for the Right Window

A spiritual coach was planning her signature group program.
The offer was complete. She was ready.
But something felt... off.

We checked her chart:

1. She was in **Saturn-Moon Dasha** (discipline + emotion)
2. **Moon was waning in Scorpio** — a time of internal clearing, not external action
3. The date she picked added to **7** — vibration of introspection, not visibility

🛑 We delayed the launch by **11 days**:

1. Moved to **Waxing Moon in Aries** (boldness, action)
2. Date vibrated to **3** — creativity and expression
3. Jupiter transited her 10th house (career)

✅ Outcome:

1. 12 program spots filled
2. 3 extra joined the waitlist
3. Her visibility and peace both increased

"Delaying my launch was hard… but it gave me success without strain." — *her words*

📅 Numerology Launch Date Guide

Use this table to select the best **energetic day vibration** for launches, events, or new projects:

Date Vibration	Meaning	Ideal For…
1	Leadership	Personal brands, bold new initiatives
3	Creativity	Courses, group programs, expressive brands
5	Speed & reach	Tech, virality, digital products
6	Beauty & ease	Wellness, women-centric brands
8	Wealth & scale	Long-term projects, funding, investment
9	Service & impact	Healing, donation-based or mission-driven

⚫ Avoid launching on dates that total **2 (emotional fog)**, **4 (delays)** or **7 (detachment)** unless supported by astrology.

✨ Calculate by adding DD + MM + YYYY and reducing to 1 digit.
E.g., 12 July 2025 = 1+2+0+7+2+0+2+5 = 19 → 1 + 9 = **10 → 1**

🌑 Moon Phases: When to Move or Wait

Moon Phase	Energetic Meaning	Best For...
New Moon	Seeding new energy	Intentions, internal clarity
Waxing Moon	Expansion, visibility builds	Launching, marketing, outreach
Full Moon	Peak visibility + completion	Events, reveals, bold actions
Waning Moon	Releasing, retreat	Rebranding, reflection, healing
Eclipse Days	Karmic chaos	Avoid all launches unless clearing work

Best window: **Waxing Moon + Vibration 1, 3, 5, or 8**

🪔 Launch Day Energetic Activation Ritual

Before going live with a new offer, product, or event:

🌟 Do this ritual on launch morning:

1. Face **East** at sunrise or 11:11 AM
2. Place your logo, offer doc, or sales page in front of you
3. Light a diya or white candle
4. Say aloud:

*"I release this offering with love, clarity, and grace.
May it reach every soul it is meant to serve."*

5. Chant:

"Om Aim Hreem Kleem Namah" (108x)
(Mantra of clarity, attraction, and fulfillment)

6. Bless your laptop or phone with rose water or a white flower
7. Launch. Trust. Let go.

🛑 When to Delay — Even If You're Ready

Sometimes, the energy says "wait." Honor it.

Sign to Pause	What It Indicates
You feel tired, anxious, or "foggy"	Internal resistance or wrong alignment
Moon is waning in water signs	Emotional heaviness — low buyer response
Date vibration = 4 or 7	Delay, karmic testing, no buzz
Dasha period is Rahu–Moon	Illusion, buyer confusion, energy leaks
Big launch overlaps Mercury retrograde	Tech glitches, unclear communication

Wait 3–7 days. Let the clouds pass.
Your creation deserves **a sky that supports it**.

💥 Closing Quote

"In business, timing isn't luck.
It's **alignment with rhythm.**
The cosmos already knows when your light should shine.
Wait for the moment when visibility feels effortless."

Launch less. Align more.
Because the right timing is the loudest marketing strategy of all.

📕 Chapter 8: Energetic Branding

Subheading: How to Design a Brand That Speaks Before You Do

"Your brand isn't just visual.
It's vibrational.
People feel your frequency before they read a single word."
— *Shantulya Saini*

🌀 What Is Energetic Branding?

Most entrepreneurs build brands using:

1. Market research
2. Color theory
3. Funnel advice

But few consider the most powerful question:

❓ Does my brand match my **soul signature**?

Your **brand is your energetic ambassador**.
It speaks on your behalf when you're not in the room.
Every color, shape, font, and name emit a vibration — either **attracting aligned clients** or repelling them subtly.

💡 Real Story: From Invisible to Magnetic

A therapist-turned-healer came to me with a brand that "just didn't feel right."

Her website:

1. Used **gray, brown, and maroon**
2. Fonts were blocky and rigid
3. Logo was a **sharp-edged square with no curves**

Despite offering transformation, her energy online felt… flat.

Her inner energy = soft, safe, divine feminine

Her visual energy = hard, old-school, masculine

We made 3 changes:

1. Introduced **rose pink + gold** (vibration 6 + 1 = luxury + leadership)
2. Switched to a **script-style font** (approachable, feminine)
3. Changed the logo to a **circular lotus mandala** (wholeness, softness, sacredness)

Within **3 weeks**:

1. Website engagement doubled
2. A past client reached out saying, *"Your site feels like healing now."*
3. She booked 2 new clients without changing her service

She didn't rewrite her words.
She rewrote her **brand frequency**.

🎨 Color Vibrations: Your Brand's Emotional Aura

Each color holds a specific vibrational field — numerologically and spiritually.

Color	Vibration	Symbolism & Brand Use
🔴 Red	1	Boldness, action, initiation — coaching, startups
🟠 Orange	3	Joy, creativity, movement — workshops, events
🟡 Yellow	5	Expansion, learning, play — tech, education
🟢 Green	6	Heart, healing, calm — wellness, female brands
🔵 Blue	2 / 4	Trust, depth, strategy — law, finance, clarity
🟣 Purple	7	Spiritual insight — metaphysics, intuitive brands
⚫ Black	8	Power, luxury — premium, coaching, CEOs
🤍 White	9	Purity, transformation — non-profits, spiritual orgs

Choose **primary + secondary** colors that reflect your *soul + client resonance.*

🔺 Logo Shape Symbolism

Shape	Energy Vibe	Ideal For...
⚫ Circle	Flow, oneness, divine	Healing, feminine brands, heart-led biz
🔺 Triangle ↑	Fire, drive, ambition	Startups, bold launches, leadership
🔻 Triangle ↓	Feminine, intuition	Womb-based brands, spirituality
⬛ Square	Structure, logic	Law, finance, disciplined brands
🌀 Spiral	Evolution, soul work	Coaches, teachers, retreat leaders
♾️ Infinity	Timelessness, harmony	Lifestyle, product-based soul businesses

---

🔠 Fonts Have Frequency

Font Type	Energy Tone	Use For...
Serif (e.g., Times)	Classic, grounded	Authority, academic, formal
Sans Serif (e.g., Lato)	Modern, clean	Clarity, digital, tech
Script / Cursive	Feminine, emotional	Healing, luxury, lifestyle
Display / Bold	Loud, high visibility	Events, promotions, launches

🧘 Choose fonts that match your message tone and **your inner frequency**.

🌕 The Brand Aura Ritual

Monthly Brand Energy Reset (Ideal at New Moon or 1st of month)

🪔 Steps:

1. Sit with your logo, website, or product name open
2. Light a diya or incense — sandalwood or lavender
3. Play 528 Hz (heart activation) or chant "OM" slowly 9x
4. Close your eyes and visualize:

    1. Your brand color glowing
    2. Ideal clients smiling as they discover your page

5. Affirm:

"My brand is a lighthouse for those I'm meant to serve.
It transmits clarity, love, and power."

✅ This anchors your brand in intentional energy before you market it.

✅ Energetic Brand Checklist

Element	Aligned? (✓)
Brand Name numerologically aligned	
Primary color matches soul energy	
Logo shape reflects intention	
Fonts feel "like you"	
Website text feels soul-authentic	
Visuals match vibration of offer	

✔ 5–6 = High brand congruence
⚠ 3 or less = Time for a brand alignment reset

✨ Closing Affirmation

"My brand is not just a look.
It is a frequency field.
When I design in alignment, I become unforgettable — without shouting."

Let your brand become the **mirror of your mission**.
Let it speak… before you do.

📕 Chapter 9: Spiritual Sales Flow

Subheading: Selling with Soul, Not Struggle

"Sales is not about persuasion.
It's about permission — to share your soul's gift with those who are ready."
— *Shantulya Saini*

💡 The Truth About Selling

Most founders carry unspoken guilt around selling.

They feel:

1. "What if I'm bothering people?"
2. "What if I sound greedy?"
3. "What if they say no?"

These thoughts **block your frequency** — and clients can feel it.

Sales is not about convincing.
It's about **inviting**.
It's about **energy exchange** — when your offering meets their soul's readiness.

💡 Real Story: From Selling to Serving

Meera, a spiritual business coach, came to me saying:

"I know my offer helps people. But when it's time to sell, I freeze."

She had:

1. A polished ₹22,000 coaching package
2. Happy past clients
3. But zero response to her last 3 Instagram posts

Energetic Audit:

1. Her **voice while selling** felt hesitant and apologetic
2. Her **offer price** = 4 vibration (resistance, karmic testing)

3. She was under **Ketu–Moon Dasha** (fog, withdrawal)

Frequency Fix:

✅ We:

1. Changed price to ₹25,555 (→ 6 = harmony, Venus)
2. Wrote a new call-to-action: *"If you're feeling the pull, I'd love to guide you."*
3. Did a **Heart-Centered Sales Ritual** (below) before going live
4. Practiced energetic **receiving visualization** for 3 days

☑ Within 4 days, she sold 2 packages with no DM pushing.

🎯 Sales Block → Energy Shift Table

Inner Block Thought	How It Shows Up	Frequency Shift
"What if they can't afford it?"	You downplay your value	"Those meant for this will feel ready."
"I need to be convincing."	Overexplaining, chasing energy	"My clarity is the invitation."
"Sales = pressure"	You avoid pitching	"Sales = sacred service"
"I'll be judged if I charge this"	Pricing shame, discounting	"My price reflects energetic exchange."

Your beliefs shape your **sales aura.**

🧘 Heart-Centered Sales Ritual

Do this before a big offer drop, DM conversation, or webinar/pitch.

🪔 Steps:

1. Light a candle and sit with hand over your heart
2. Breathe deeply and repeat:

"I now open my field to receive aligned souls ready for this transformation."

3. Visualize people smiling and saying "Yes" with ease

4. Bless your phone, Zoom link, or sales page with rose water or sandalwood

5. Say: - "This offer is my service. May it find those it is meant to serve."

📌 Pro tip: Do this once a day during open cart or discovery call week.

💼 Soul-Led Sales Strategy Tips

Practice	Energetic Benefit
Sell on **Waxing Moon** or Friday (Venus)	Opens receiving + attraction channels
Use vibration-aligned price (1, 5, 6, 8)	Resonates with wealth and worthiness
Share **stories > stats**	Builds emotional safety and trust
Allow silence in DMs/discovery calls	Gives space for soul decisions
Use phrases like: *"If this resonates..."* *"You'll know if this is meant for you"*	Activates intuitive buying — not logic traps

---

🛍️ Your Sales Energy Checklist

Statement	Check (✓)
I feel grounded, not desperate, while selling	
My pricing feels honest and energetically clean	
I trust my people will find me at the right time	
My offer feels like a gift I'm proud to share	
I speak about my offer with emotion, not pressure	

✔ 5 = You're in spiritual sales alignment
⚠ 3 or less = Do the ritual, recheck vibration, and pause

🌟 Final Affirmation

"Selling is not separate from my purpose.
It is a sacred invitation to serve.
The souls who need me are already feeling the call —
I simply open the door."

📘 <u>Chapter 10: Inner Work & Intuition for Founders</u>

<u>Subheading: Building Your Business from the Inside Out</u>

"You can't lead a soul-aligned business with a disconnected soul."
— *Shantulya Saini*

🧘 Why Inner Work is Not Optional

You've built your pitch deck.
You've followed strategy.
You've hired coaches, marketers, or mentors.

But if you haven't asked:

"What is *my energy* creating behind the scenes?"
Then your business is still being built on sand.

Behind every repeated pattern in business —
❌ self-sabotage
❌ burnout
❌ wrong hires
❌ stuck launches
— there's often an **unconscious wound, belief, or energetic block** waiting to be met.

Your business doesn't just need structure.
It needs **spiritual stability**.
And that begins with you.

💡 Real Story: Hiring from Wound vs. Wisdom

Tanya, a purpose-led founder, couldn't understand why she kept hiring the wrong people.
Team members who didn't care. Missed deadlines. Emotional outbursts.

She told me, *"I'm doing everything right on paper. Why does this keep happening?"*

We went within:

1. She discovered an old subconscious belief:
   "If I am supported, I will be abandoned."

2. Her childhood experience had wired her to **repel deep support**

3. Her outer decisions reflected her **inner fear of trusting anyone fully**

Through 21 days of:

1. Inner child journaling
2. Silent decision-making practices
3. Throat chakra clearing

She began choosing with clarity.

Her next hire?
A grounded, intuitive project manager who stayed — and scaled — with her for 3 years.

Her business didn't need a recruiter.
It needed **emotional reprogramming.**

🧭 Intuition vs. Fear: Which One Is Leading?

So many founders confuse **gut feelings** with fear reactions.
Let's decode:

Thought / Situation	FEAR Reaction	INTUITION Signature
"I'm not sure if I should hire them"	Urgency, pressure, second-guessing	Calm clarity, persistent inner nudge
"This launch feels off"	Panic, overwhelm, FOMO	Quiet discomfort or deep knowing
"Should I change this offer?"	Doubt, tension, comparing others	Light drop in energy → pull to realign
"This price feels high"	Guilt, throat tightens	Soft urge to adjust slightly, not collapse

Always ask:
"Am I choosing from **urgency** or **alignment**?"

🍃 Weekly Founder Inner Calibration Ritual

This practice reconnects you to your **soul CEO** — the one beyond logic and hustle.

🌱 Do this once a week (Monday sunrise or Friday dusk)

🧘 Steps:

1. Sit quietly with hand on heart
2. Ask:

"Where am I leading from fear, not wisdom?"
"What am I avoiding seeing in myself?"

3. Journal for 7–11 minutes — free writing, no filters
4. Pull a tarot card or write a message from your intuition
5. Breathe deeply and say:

"I now lead from inner truth.
I trust my business is a mirror of my vibration."

🌑 Business Blocks & Their Inner Roots

Behind every outer "problem" is often a soul assignment.

Outer Block	Inner Work Trigger
Constant team drama	Control issues, fear of losing authority
Launches stuck at 70%	Fear of being seen, fear of receiving
Burnout & resentment in offers	Over giving, self-worth tied to proving
Low sales from strong content	Throat chakra block, fear of rejection
Repeated client refunds or drop-offs	Lack of boundaries, fear of being "too much"

Your shadow doesn't need shame.
It needs awareness, softness, and integration.

🧠 Intuition as Your Cofounder

The most successful founders I've coached don't just scale.
They **sense**.
They:

1. Delay launches when it feels off
2. Hire based on energy, not just CVs
3. Price from **inner permission**, not just market analysis
4. Create offers from divine downloads — and watch them sell out

You don't need to *learn* intuition.
You need to **clear the noise** that's blocking it.

✅ Soul Leadership Calibration Checklist

Reflection Prompt	**Tune In (✓)**
I take silent space before major decisions	
I journal or reflect on emotional patterns weekly	
I trust my body's signals (expansion vs. tension)	
I say "no" when something feels misaligned	
I don't outsource decisions I can soul-source	

✔ 4–5 = Intuition-aligned founder
⚠ 2 or less = Begin weekly ritual & release overthinking

💥 Final Affirmation

"My intuition is my greatest business partner.
The more I trust it, the more magnetic my vision becomes.
I no longer need permission — only presence."

📕 Chapter 12: Shadow Work for Founders

Subheading: Healing the Inner Blocks That Sabotage Outer Success

"The shadow isn't your enemy.
It's the part of you most desperate to be loved — and most afraid to be seen."
— *Shantulya Saini*

🌓 Why Every Founder Must Face Their Shadow

As a founder, you're not just building a business.
You're also projecting your:

1. Fears
2. Patterns
3. Childhood wounds
4. Ancestral karmas
   ...into every product, price, pitch, and partner.

What you don't heal in private will eventually leak in public —
through bad hires, self-sabotage, client drama, or energy crashes.

💡 Founder Story: The Shiny Mask

Ravi was a charismatic wellness startup founder.
On the surface, he was magnetic — speaking at events, attracting clients.

But behind the scenes:

1. He micromanaged his team
2. Burned out every quarter
3. Obsessed over competitors

When we explored deeper, we found:

1. A childhood story of being bullied and silenced
2. A need to **be perfect to feel safe**
3. A shadow of control masking deep fear of betrayal

Once Ravi began inner child work + journaling triggers,
he stepped back from reactive leadership...
and stepped into *regulated power*.
Revenue rose. But more importantly — **peace returned**.

🧩 The 5 Core Founder Shadows

Shadow Name	Root Wound	Business Behavior
💼 The Prover	"I must earn love."	Overdelivering, undercharging
🧠 The Perfectionist	"Mistakes = rejection."	Fear of launching, endless editing
✋ The Controller	"If I let go, I lose."	Micromanagement, burnout
🙂 The Pleaser	"If I say no, I'll be abandoned."	Weak boundaries, underpricing
🕳 The Avoider	"If I fail, I'll disappear."	Procrastination, ghosting leads

Shadow Clue:
If something in business keeps repeating — it's probably not strategy.
It's shadow.

💔 Mini Case: When Shadow Led to Collapse

A digital artist launched a course with 2,000 email subscribers.
Beautiful design. Great content.
But **only 4 people signed up.**

She spiraled: "I'm not meant for this."

Behind the scenes:

1. She feared pricing at ₹5,000, so launched at ₹799
2. Her emails said "Sorry to bother you, just in case you're interested..."
3. Her *Pleaser Shadow* dimmed her power

No one felt her conviction — so no one committed.

It wasn't failure. It was shadow.

🌑 Shadow to Light Pathway

Shadow Pattern	Awareness Tool	Light Action Step
Undervaluing offers	Journal "What am I afraid to charge?"	Increase pricing by 11%
Procrastinating launch	Track daily energy drops	Create ritual to "bless the fear"
Toxic hiring cycles	Reflect on repeated red flags	Build a values-based hire checklist
Always "fixing" client results	Notice your savior complex	Add client accountability contracts

💡 Awareness without action = insight.
Awareness + action = **alchemical shift.**

🌿 Ritual: Shadow Dialogue Practice (Weekly)

1. Sit quietly. Breathe. Ask:

"What part of me feels unsafe right now?"

2. Write as if your shadow is speaking:

"I don't trust this launch… I'm scared no one shows up."

3. Then respond from your higher self:

"I hear you. And I'm not abandoning you. Let's do this together."

✅ This builds **inner integration** — so you lead from clarity, not fragmentation.

🔮 Astro-Numerology Shadow Clues

Placement / Number	Possible Shadow
Ketu conjunct Moon	Emotional suppression, detachment
Rahu in 10th or 7th house	Obsession with validation, success
Life Path 4 or 7	Control, isolation, silent sabotage

Placement / Number	Possible Shadow
Saturn Return phase	Fear of being seen, karmic collapse

Astrology doesn't cause shadows — but it *reveals where they hide.*

📜 Shadow Work Integration Scorecard

Statement	Yes/No
I notice when I act from fear, not flow	
I don't guilt-trip myself when I pause	
I track patterns that repeat	
I take time weekly for self-inquiry	
I no longer try to "fix" everything instantly	

✔ 4–5 = You're leading from integration
⚠ 2 or less = Begin with 7-day trigger journaling challenge

💥 Closing Dual Affirmations

🌓 *Shadow Affirmation*
"I meet the parts of me I used to run from.
I see my fear, and I love it into light."

🌞 *Leadership Affirmation*
"I no longer lead with performance.
I lead with presence.
I am the medicine my business has been waiting for."

Let this chapter be your mirror.
Because when you build your business **with your shadow, not against it** —
you build something the world can trust.

📘 Chapter 13: Inner Work & Intuition for Founders

Subheading: Trusting the Wisdom That Knows Before the Data Does

"Every business has a business plan.
But every soul-led founder must have a soul plan."
— *Shantulya Saini*

🧘 Why Intuition Is Your Cofounder

Every great founder decision didn't start on a spreadsheet —
It started in the **gut**, the **vision**, the **quiet knowing**.

Strategy scales.
Intuition **aligns**.

Yet many founders:

1. Outsource hard decisions
2. Follow "best practices" that feel wrong
3. Suppress intuitive nudges as "unproven"

And so they end up **misaligned**, burnt out, or stuck in analysis.

💡 Real Story: When Ignoring Intuition Cost More Than a Pivot

Sohini, a conscious product founder, had built a 5K waitlist.
Her coach told her to "go all-in" on launching in Q2.
But she had a strange inner resistance. She felt foggy. Unsettled.

Still, she pushed forward...
→ Launch flopped
→ Inventory stuck
→ She fell ill for 3 weeks

Only later did she discover:

1. She was in **Moon–Rahu Dasha**
2. It was an **eclipse window**
3. And her inner voice had *warned* her all along

When she relaunched 3 months later — in alignment —
She sold out 70% in 48 hours.

*"My intuition didn't need proof.
It needed permission."* — she now says

🔄 Inner Sourcing vs. Outsourcing

Decision Type	Outsourced Energy	Inner-Sourced Frequency
Offer creation	"What are others doing?"	"What transformation lights me up?"
Pricing	"What's the market rate?"	"What feels clean and confident?"
Hiring	"Their CV is great."	"Do I feel safe and supported?"
Scaling	"I *should* scale now."	"Is this aligned with my nervous system?"
Saying no	"What will they think?"	"Does this feel off in my body?"

Your intuition speaks in:

1. Energy
2. Sensation
3. Symbols
4. Dreams
5. Silence

🧰 Intuition Activation Toolkit

Use these tools to sharpen your business sixth sense:

1. 🃏 3-Card Founder Tarot Spread

1. **Card 1:** Where I am now
2. **Card 2:** What I'm not seeing
3. **Card 3:** My next aligned action

→ Use before launches, hiring, or rebranding

---

2. ▯ Dream Decoder

Keep a small journal by your bed. Ask before sleeping:

"What is my next right move?"

Look for:

1. Recurring symbols (water = flow, fire = urgency)
2. People from past = inner patterns reactivating
3. Rooms = your inner energetic layout

---

3. 👂 Daily Intuition Ritual (5 mins)

1. Sit silently in the morning or after meditation
2. Place hand on belly
3. Ask:

"What do I need to know today?"

4. Write the first 3 words, images, or feelings that arise

Trust what comes — even if it makes no sense yet.

🔁 When to Pause and Listen

If you feel:

1. Constant mental noise
2. Spinning in indecision
3. Launches that feel "off"
4. Team or client misfires

Pause.
Breathe.
Turn inward.

Your soul is not unclear.
It's often just **crowded out** by noise.

🌟 Final Integration: Business Meets Inner Voice

Use this flow every week or before big decisions:

Moment	Action
Feeling stuck	Do the 3-card spread or journal "What am I afraid to hear?"
Big launch coming	Check Moon phase + gut + dream signs
Team conflict	Meditate on: "What truth am I avoiding?"
Client misalignment	Breathe into your body → where is the discomfort?
New idea download	Write it → speak it aloud → does it light you up?

🔮 Final Affirmation

"I no longer ask for permission to feel what I feel.
My inner knowing is not random — it is my strategy.
I build my business by listening within...
And what I create from soul — becomes unstoppable."

Let your data confirm what your **soul already knows.**

Your intuition is not your backup plan.
It's your business blueprint in disguise.

📕 Chapter 14: Spiritual Sales Flow

Subheading: Selling as Sacred Service — Not Survival

"Selling isn't convincing. It's transmitting.
When your frequency is clean, the 'yes' becomes natural."
— *Shantulya Saini*

🎯 Why Sales Feels "Sticky" to Soul-Led Founders

You know your offer is powerful.
You've seen transformation.
But when it comes time to sell… you hesitate.

You think:

1. "What if they can't afford it?"
2. "What if I sound pushy?"
3. "What if they say no?"

Here's the truth:
Sales blocks rarely come from your offer.
They come from **your aura during the ask.**

💡 Founder Story #1: Meera's Magnetic Shift

Meera, a spiritual coach, was launching her 3-month healing program.
She felt deeply connected to her work — but froze when selling.

She whispered instead of owning her price. She added bonuses to "justify."
Nothing sold.

We discovered:

1. She was in a **Moon–Ketu Dasha** (fog, people-pleasing)
2. Her ₹22,000 price added to a **4** (karmic debt)
3. Her body tensed when saying her CTA aloud

✅ We shifted:

1. Price to ₹25,555 (vibration 6 = harmony, ease)
2. Added a heart-centered ritual before showing up online
3. Rewrote her CTA: *"If your soul is whispering yes, I'm here to walk with you."*

4 clients in 5 days. No urgency. No push.

💔 Founder Story #2: Trapped in Undervaluing

Vishal, a mindfulness coach, launched his group workshop for ₹299.
He said, *"I want it to be accessible."*

Result:

1. No one showed up
2. He felt drained
3. A few people who joined never participated

What went wrong?

He priced from **guilt**, not guidance.

"When your price doesn't match your energy, it attracts confusion, not conversion."

Later, he priced at ₹5,500 — with the same content —
and filled all spots with committed souls.

🧠 Pricing with Power: Energy + Logic Blend

1. ✅ Tune into: *What feels clean, clear, and honest in my body?*
2. 📊 Check market ranges — but don't collapse into them
3. 🔢 Use price vibrations:
    1. 1, 5, 6, or 8 = activation, expansion, harmony, wealth
    2. Avoid 4 or 7 unless spiritually relevant

A clean price carries **confidence, clarity, and command.**

🔄 Sales Block → Energy Shift Table

Inner Thought	What It Creates	Shift to...
"People can't afford me."	Attracts scarcity	"Aligned souls are ready to invest."
"I need to prove it's worth it."	Overcompensating, fatigue	"My offer is already enough."
"Sales = pressure."	Avoidance, poor CTA	"Sales = sacred invitation."
"High prices = greed."	Guilt, low boundaries	"High prices honor time and energy."

✨ 5-Step Heart-Centered Sales Alignment Ritual

Do this before any launch, pitch, or discovery call week.

🌼 Steps:

1. **Silence & Intent (2 mins)**
   Place your hands on your chest. Ask:

"Who is this offer meant to serve today?"

2. **Bless Your Offer (1 min)**
   Light a diya or candle beside your sales page/logo.

3. **Say Aloud**:

"This offering is a vehicle of healing.
It will find the hearts that are ready."

4. **Receive Visualization (3 mins)**
   Picture 3 joyful, soul-aligned clients discovering your offer and saying "Yes!"

5. **Walk Away with Gratitude**
   Let the energy do its work. No pushing.

💡 *Sales happens before they click. It happens in your frequency.*

📈 Energetic Sales Strategy Tips

Aligned Sales Practice	Energetic Impact
Launch on **Friday or Waxing Moon**	Activates Venus (attraction)
Use phrases like "If this resonates…"	Encourages intuition-based decisions
Pause after offering — don't overtalk	Allows aligned decision to surface
Share story, not stats	Emotion is the buying engine
Price with numerology in mind	Locks in energetic support

📜 Sales Self-Check: Are You Aligned?

Statement	Check (✓)
I feel peaceful when I present my price	
My CTA (call to action) feels natural to say aloud	
I don't pressure myself to chase leads	
My offer feels like a gift, not a gamble	
I celebrate "No" as much as "Yes"	

✔ 4–5 = Your sales frequency is clear
⚠ 3 or less = Do ritual + check pricing vibration

💬 Wisdom from the Masters

"I don't sell. I serve. And when people feel served, they want more."
— *Oprah Winfrey*

🌟 Final Affirmation

"Selling is an extension of my love.
My voice is a vessel. My energy is the bridge.
I don't chase — I attract, serve, and receive with joy."

📘 Chapter 15: Energetic Branding & Digital Vibration

Subheading: Crafting an Online Presence That Speaks Before You Do

"Your brand is not just what they see.
It's what they **feel** before they read a single word."
— *Shantulya Saini*

🌐 Why Your Online Presence is Energetic First

People don't buy your product first.
They buy your **frequency**.

Your Instagram, website, or logo isn't just visual — it's **vibrational**.

Every font, word, photo, and color carry **a signature**.
It either draws your soul client in... or silently repels them.

💡 Founder Story: The Brand That Finally Spoke Her Soul

Aditi ran a beautiful healing practice — in real life, she glowed.
But her Instagram felt... cold. Generic. Flat.

She said, *"People say they like my vibe, but my page doesn't get engagement."*

We reviewed her digital vibration:

1. Black and maroon grid (vibration = heaviness, Saturn energy)
2. Font: bold caps (too masculine)
3. Bio number = 7 (detachment, mystery)
4. Post tone: passive, over-explaining, no soul story

We shifted:

1. Colors to rose pink, white, and soft gold (Venus + Moon combo)
2. Fonts to flowing script + soft sans-serif
3. Bio reworded to a **6-vibration** line: *"Helping women heal gently with light + soul"*
4. Chakra-informed highlight covers
5. Weekly *digital aura cleanse* using mantras before posting

Result:
✅ Engagement 3x in 3 weeks
✅ DMs flowed in with "Your page just feels safe"
✅ She said: *"Now my brand feels like a blessing, not a battle."*

🎯 The Energetic Branding Map

Element	**Frequency Role**
Name / Domain	Identity + throat chakra clarity
Fonts	Masculine = bold, clear / Feminine = flowing, soft
Brand Colors	Each tied to chakra + numerology
Bio/Tagline	Energy code — test vibration via Chaldean
Content Voice	Expression energy — Is it calm, chaotic, unclear?
Photo Vibe	Are your visuals transmitting emotion or editing?

🌈 Chakra-Based Color Branding

Chakra	**Color**	**Brand Vibe**
Root	Red	Power, urgency, survival — startup, hustle
Sacral	Orange	Creativity, joy — content, fashion
Solar	Yellow	Optimism, clarity — coaching, communication
Heart	Green	Trust, healing — wellness, feminine brands
Throat	Blue	Communication, truth — consulting, media
Third Eye	Indigo	Intuition, insight — spiritual teachers
Crown	Purple/White	Divinity, cosmic — mystics, visionary brands

---

🔢 Numerology for Digital Assets

Element	Tip to Align Frequency
Instagram Handle	Reduce to single digit using Chaldean numerology
Website Domain	Use brand name vibration = 1, 5, 6, or 8
Email ID	Avoid double repeating harsh numbers (e.g., 4, 7)

💡 *Pro tip:* Test your full Instagram URL in numerology
→ e.g., "instagram.com/your handle" → sum total

📱 High-Frequency Online Presence Checklist

Prompt	Check (✓)
Do my photos, fonts, and colors reflect my soul work?	
Is my brand's message easy to receive in 7 seconds?	
Does my Instagram bio match my vibration intention?	
Do I post from overflow — not desperation or guilt?	
Have I cleared my feed of expired or misaligned energy?	

✔ 5 = You're broadcasting your soul clearly
⚠ 3 or less = It's time to tune your digital vibration

🔮 Ritual: Weekly Digital Aura Cleanse

Do this every Sunday or Friday morning:

1. Sit with your phone/laptop on a white cloth
2. Light a diya or incense (lavender or sandalwood)
3. Chant "OM Shreem Kleem Namah" 21x
4. Wipe phone screen with rosewater
5. Delete one expired post, email, or draft that feels "off"

6. Bless your page with:

"May my presence call in the souls I'm meant to serve."

🌙 Planetary Influence on Visibility

1. 🌕 **Full Moon** = peak views, visibility burst (great for storytelling)
2. 📅 **Friday (Venus)** = love, attraction, ideal for launch posts
3. 🧠 **Mercury transit** = speak, pitch, go live
4. 🚫 **Eclipse season / Mercury retrograde** = review, reflect, don't force

Track **Dasha periods** too — visibility flows better in **Venus, Jupiter, Sun**, not Rahu–Ketu unless deeply spiritual.

💥 Final Affirmation

"My online presence is a portal.
I no longer post to prove. I post to transmit.
My frequency speaks louder than strategy — and those who are ready, always feel it."
